A SHORT BOOK *of* POETRY AND THOUGHTS *to* SHARE

MARYANNE WRIGHT

Ordering Information:

Prime Seven Media
518 Landmann St.
Tomah City, WI 54660

Printed in the United States of America

TABLE OF CONTENTS

This book is dedicated to my children –
Nicholas and Lauren.

Introduction

For lovers, dreamers, and those that weep, all have parts in this book to read. For I have been and seen such things and still am experiencing all life can bring.

This short book of poetry and thoughts has been written through Covid and alludes to happier times when we were naive to think that we could depend upon the world staying as it was.

MY LOVE

When you have sun light, I have the moon.

When for me new leaves grow, you are seeing them fall.

With many miles and days apart, I reach across the stars, to touch your heart.

When your eyes are closed my chosen one, my heart beats right over yours.

A night serene, calm, then woken by a golden kiss from the sun.

Time and tide won't reach you in time, only dreams thrown to the stars.

Travel to my love fast, by wings of night and let the sun bring it to life.

WHAT IS LOVE?

Is it a thing that melts the ice from my eyes
when he smiles at me?

Or does it make my bones dissolve,
when he walks up close?
Is it when he burns my body with his fleeting touch?

Or is it the feeling of extreme pain when I awake alone
from a dream of being with him?

Is it a thing that I can place in a jar, to preserve it,
to spoon some on my bread when hungry?
Can it be in the song that whispers to me in
the light of dawn?

What is love?

PIECES OF YOUR LOVE

Love in little pieces, are given to me in bags of brown paper and cardboard boxes.

Flowers grown from your soil, are picked and wrapped for me to enjoy.

Their silken petals are like your soft kisses.

I brush them over my lips and experience their sensual joy.

These all grew in the soil that your feet walked in.

Where your thoughts stuck to the buds to be transferred to my lips.

These little gifts from your heart are honey to my soul.

BIRTH

So fragile, transparent emerging from
your hanging sheath.

Wings crumpled, wet and blue with black, slowly
unfolding, away from the suspended death.

For the first time, with breezes full of perfume,
you take your breath.

Wings fully dried, and legs holding onto the leaf,
you begin to move your wings to practice your flight.

Iridescence catches in your wings and is so bright.

Your sleek black body craves for your first feed and
trembles with need.

Up into the sky your wings lift you on the first breeze,
your maiden flight begins.

THE LAST GOODBYE

I feel the golden warmth of the afternoon hug my
shoulders, like you used to in your brown leather chair.

Sunlight dapples the gum and starkly white the trunk
shines.
I watch the fountain of water from the waterfall,
stream down the windows, creating a myriad
of reflecting rainbows.

The air holds the scent of gum and roses.
Your carnations add to the essence.

Up front of the room on the pulpit, I see light dancing
across the polished wood. Its trail gradually follows the
rainbows one by one.

The flowers on your casket nod farewell, as you are
moved slowly away.

Red curtains close around your frame, and you are taken.

I close my eyes and think of you, willing your face to see.

I kiss your image again and feel your hand on my
shoulder, touching me as a last goodbye.

OCTOBER

So, open your centers, release your heady scent. The sun is shining, warm air blows across my face.

Petals, new, glossy yellow, have sweet scents of fresh life. A tangy mix of cinnamon and sugar, inviting, tantalizing bees from hives.

Bluebells and Hawthorne are out by the woods and the air is calling, "come sample my goods".

Fresh mown hay, pungent sweet to the nose, scents my hair as I ride past hedgerows.

It beckons, "come, wait awhile, roll in my rows. Cover yourself and be one with all growth".

A bank of Jasmine can be smelt for miles, as I suddenly spy its star shaped flowers. Bees drunk from its nectar, legs full of pollen, are trying to fly with such a burden.

The woods are open, and I enter within, a rich smell of green, a heaven within.

The Tui, its plume white on its chin, is singing to its mate in branches green. A Fantail follows behind, as I stir up midges for it to snap. Its cheeky dancing all around my head, as it feeds itself and keeps with my pace.

SPRING

Slowly, steadily, it climbs, breaking its soft brown bed
towards the light.
Soil and dead leaves part as its tips reveal green, stark
against the earth so dark.

A gentle rain waters the ground and fills the puddles and
the fields. Trees with branches so bare and cold, take a
hue of bright gold.
Sap has risen, buds are swollen, their cases tender and
throw their pollens.

Snowdrops cover the ground below competing with
violets in knots of colour.
Blackbirds arrange themselves in the branches vying for
the attention of their partners.
The air no longer wears the scent of mold and cold, but of
sweet vibrance of verdance so bold.

SUMMER AT THE BEACH

Diamonds sparkle in the sand and waves glint their unyielded treasure.

Heat on my back, then she licks at my legs.

I touch and cup the foam with my hands, frothy like bubble bath. The wind teases through my shirt and dances solo with my hair.

Wading through the waves that suck at my feet, splashing my thighs and shorts.

All is blue and white spume. The deepest of summer blue to a pale reflection to the distant shores.

The air tastes of seaweed and salt and a hint of heat. I stick out my tongue and taste its scents.

Tern's fly, their white silhouette above reflects on the sand. Their lonely calls cut the air, crying at the mermaids that have invaded their spots.

Along the shoreline, follows the tide and treasures given up by the sea. The flotsam and jetson are the bounties from the sea.

My face to the sun, my eyes half closed, all is well, I feel free.

SUMMER AT HOME

Sweat trickling down my back wetting my dress, much too thin to absorb the rest.

Legs bare and moving in a pace, with the slow beat of the bass.

Grass warm and dry underfoot, as toes hold the balance in a dance.

Head tilted backwards, eyes closed, enjoying this moment on my toes. Arms outstretched, hands moving to the drums, its bliss dancing in the hot summer sun.

Humming the song and forgetting all else, just giving my body to its clasp.

Warm sun touching my skin, music clasping my soul from within. My innocent sin.

AUTUMN

Soft golden light seeps through the hedgerow, brightening Hawthorn berries voluptuous red. Grasses growing underneath are sunburnt yellow from summer past. Crisp golden leaves cover the meadow, where in summer daisies nodded their heads.

Old mother hedgehog is bold today, searching for a safe hideaway. She snuffles around the fens, searching for a hole to sleep. Until she spies a dry space for her to curl and keep.

The moon rises full and white, a pale globe in the light. Up ahead a skein of ducks is moving for the march, intent on feeding before the dark.

Very soon the air will thin, and Jack Frost will march in.

Nights will stay longer and frighten the day, holding the creatures as they lay.

AUTUMN LEAVES

It's crisp and crunchy underfoot, my breath frosty and plumy white, and moves before me in the light.

Trees sparkle with thousand lanterns of dew, letting loose their leaves to fly, twirling, gliding, floating by.

The brown earth receives its treasure from above and holds it with a soft caress, like velvet gloves.

Golden light plays between the leaves, peeks to spotlight the scene beneath.

Reds, russets, ambers, brilliant gold, like jewels in a treasure cask so brown, opens to reveal its boon, each leaf fashioned to display their folds, frills, and curls.

Scents of leaves mixed with damp undergrowth bring to the air mold and decay. The pungent smell of toadstools release as they spore, giving to the ground to store.

Before the frost and ice cover will shroud the earth, lace skeletons show their worth.
Such beauty and sweetness, as the trees sigh away their summers and wait with suspended breath for the call of their lady Spring.

WINTER SILENCE

Softly like black velvet sliding on the floor, snowflakes fall.

Nothing is moving, all is serene, the throb of my pulse is deafening.

Not a twig movement, not a snap, silence surrounds me like a glove.

A false blanket of white traps the ground.

Not a rustle nor sound can be heard.

My frosty breathing is loud to my ears as white silence hushes the earth.

FOG

Creeping, rolling stealthily climbing, in from the sea and onto the land.

Covering the valley in a soft blanket, the highest mountain separated from land.

Sounds of the twilight deliberately muffled, a colourful canvas the sun says good night.

The last blush of light slowly fades from my sight, leaving a grey void to greet the night.

BASKETS

Basket of happiness,
Basket of joy,

Basket of flowers brought in by my boy.

Soft little hands holding onto the handles, with wet
chubby cheeks sporting faint dimples.

Eyes shining bright through long fair lashes.
Smile so wide it covers my vision.

He comes to me, with "These are for you Mummy, I picked
them special".
He hands me daisies stalks crumpled and broken and a
love so pure, given as token.

Such a gesture of love so plain and simple, brought tears
to my eyes, I am smitten.

MY SON

The light plays with his lashes and warms his skin.

His breathing is deep and sweet on my face.

A contented smile touches the corners of his mouth.

While you are wrapped in my arms, where are you dreaming my little man?

Of fishing in the stars, in your soft blue bed that sails through the clouds, that touches the moon and sifts stardust in your net.

A tiny murmur and a half sigh, oh my, did you let a star slip by.

THE SPRITE

Climbing into the base, her little legs struggling to lift over the lip, she balanced and jumped into the fountain.

Her blue pants darkened by the wet spray. Legs wet and shiny with trickles of water.

Lifting her arms above her head, she ran, with fingers splayed towards the jets from the dolphin's grin.

She danced, her skin glistening with droplets of spray. Standing in the fountain jets her clothes soaked, my Fey child of May.

Half turning her head, she then caught my eye.
Slowly, a smile touched her mouth, then she laughed.
Her laughter sounded like church bells on a Sunday.

Her long fair hair, glistened like spun gold, splayed behind and captured the rainbow in her strands.

A moment caught in time, sheer joy to watch, such gay abandon, my daughter in play.

BREAKING AWAY

Oh, the ecstasy of starting to climb. Holding hands, sharing this journey. Strong and supple our bodies take on this walk.

Being close and stopping along the way, for the other to take a breath. Laughing and singing as we round corners, still climbing, climbing, climbing,

Such pretty baubles doth life bring, to decorate our tent. So soft a bed to lay together, to watch the stars.

Child likenesses of us we bring to share, such happiness and joy to love. Giving them comfort and holding their hand. And still we climb.

The thrill of sharing ourselves as we explore and climb, each following the other never tiring, always climbing.

Separate steps now they find, and paths meet up along the way, each climbing.

The hands now hold the rocks and steady us, as the path has become too steep for two. Still, we climb. It is not joyous no laughter

is heard along the way. The sound of our own voices is only heard, as each of us has found the solidary path.

I am not climbing. I have stopped.

SUSPENSE

Thoughts twisting turning twirling and knotting, being held captive and constantly fretting.

Squeezing eyes shut and holding my breath, I wait for the anger to erupt from your head.

Treading on tip toes across the room, I hope you don't notice where I am headed.
I sneak outside and let out my breath, that was so close I almost fainted.

The knife in my back slowly fades away and deep breathing helps steady my nerves.

Walking on eggshells, trying not to break, constantly keeping a smile on my face.

Showing the world what the world wants to see, has left just the mask not the person in me.

THE RACE

Flags fluttering like my pulse.
The trickle of sweat moving down my neck.

Holding my breath for a brief pause, giving furtive looks
around the track.

The crack of the start gun pops my fears and off I go,
wind whistles past my ears.

My legs feel on fire and my lungs will burst. I must past
the leader, or all will be lost.

Screwing shut my eyes; I push my body forward,
hoping my legs will keep their stride.

I am breathing in fire, too hard to swallow.
I am almost there, just one more push.

Yes, I have done it! Keep going, keep going,
Arms outstretched, smile is wide, the finish line is under
my stride.

THE LAST DRAGON

He sits alone on his crag surrounded by cool misty clouds.
His eyes are closed; head is bent under his wing in deep
repose.

The first rays of sun peer through the mist and linger
fleetingly on his nose.

The morning beckons him with rainbows of dew drops
and warms his scales.

He lifts his head and opens one eye to view his desolate
phyllite domain.

He throws back his head and a rumble is heard from his
veins.

Greeting the dawn with an elegant bow and opens his
wings for a morning soar.
Lifting his legs, he thrusts forward and throws his head
back and roars.
Over and over, he circles and glides with eyes fierce with
wildness and glee, his body weightless.

LAST DRAGON OF EVEN MORE

He sat with hunched shoulders and gazed his domain with golden eyes. Baring one tooth, he deeply sighed.

The wind around the crags was harsh and whispered of glacier fed rivers.

He gazed and searched around the valley for life.

Alas, he only was to remain and to live his days in solitary time.

The sun shone on his scales so bronze and made his chest a burst with flame.

With a roar he lifted his head and threw back his mane of scaled red hue, then spread his wings and off he flew.

Searching for prey, mate or foe, his watchful gaze searched valleys below. Until he spied movement below and spiraled towards his target.

He spied a young boy with hair so fair and eating fruit from an orchard.

He landed so lightly making no noise and waited for boy to catch his eye.

The boy intent on his pear, did not notice this beast so large. Until the boy threw his core into his direction. Arm frozen from sheer fright, mouth open, with his last bite, each eyed each other with suspicion and fright.

The boy then smiled and held out his hand and walked towards this beast so grand.

The dragon saw this brave child and decided to befriend him. He lowered his head for boy to touch and whispered that he would not harm him. Dragon felt the touch on his nose and his loneliness craved the affection. Boy could see how much beast liked this petting and attention.

Dragon and boy sat close together, and boy fed him. Dragon liked the taste of pear and thanked him.

Dragon and boy became fast friends, and each would visit the other. As summers past, boy grew up and became the village warrior.

Warrior could be seen on dragon's back flying towards the battles.

Sword in hand, shield on side, defending turf and water.

Dragon and warrior lived their days inseparable not forgotten and to this day their fables have become immortal.

THE GARDEN

The new morning was washed a pastel hue across the gray sky. Fat raindrops plopped their crystal shimmers on the lawn.

I watched the spiders web transform into a diamond studded net. The spider long gone to a cosy eave.

Even the mist had a soft sparkle to its mantle.

The garden was breathing its first deep breath after night.

I watched the sky become a soft pink blush and the brown silhouettes of the bare trees, were starkly contrasted with the softness of the day. I fancied shapes of tree men in their branches and almost saw them move towards the dawn.
The moon hung above redundant, but still not quite relinquishing its hold.

A blackbird began to sing to herald the dawn, his song a sweet tease to the light to stay and listen.

The moment was suspended in the notes.

THE STREAM

The stream sparked and shone with light trapped in the flow and current of such might.
The worn brown stones were slick with wear.

Fish swam languidly in the bottom where waters were still, waiting for a minnow to alight on the surface and be dragged downwards by the deceptive current.

A dragon fly helicoptered around looking for an overhanging leaf to launch itself down. Its wings translucent and catching the rainbow of light, like a crystal shining in the sun.

I squinted into the shimmer of sun on waters, so crystal and pure from the touch of man.

The light reflected onto my face and briefly saw a sparkle in the mud beneath. It was a small coin left by a wisher of dreams.

I left the coin as it was, as disturbing its place would seem so wrong. Dream wisher, who gave to this stream, I hope your wish was granted foreseen.

THE SUN

Here She comes!

She arises from the sea the palest of pink, carrying on her aura the faint scents of the Pacific and warm spices of the night.

Her long golden tendrils flick over the tops of the highest mountains, cascading into the crevice's; the lightest of light.

Her touch slowly melting the frosts on the grasses.

A misty coverlet rises to wrap around her nakedness, softening her outline.

Her pink silhouette still in plain sight.

As she starts to climb, her body burns her coverlet exposing her fullness, no longer in softened light.

Exposed in full, she begins her slow climb.

That delicate pink has changed to brazen gold, too intense to look on her loveliness; too harsh to gaze upon.

Directly above me her heat radiates, and it licks my skin with a silken tongue, hot, salty and full of lust.

She sucks at my energy, leaving me drained and lightheaded.

Her power grows as she moves and confronts me, her vision burning my eyes and forehead.

I squint to avoid her invading brilliance.

Turning my back to her, I carry on working, still aware of her hot embrace.

No longer in her morning gown, naked in her fierceness, her smile is cruel, and her intention to burn with ferociousness is all over her face.

I move into the shade for brief respite from her full-blown sight.

She moves slowly towards my horizon, her body is full, a deep blood orange, her smile no longer holds malice but with a soft sweet caress.

She takes in the days perfume of the soils and rivers and carries it with her to a far-off place.

The motes dance in the air above the vegetable patch in the late afternoon sky. Their crazy random patterns can be traced.

As she sinks towards her liquid bed, her golden hair splayed around her head, fanning out in the western sky. Night of black velvet closes her curtains and says goodnight, she begins her sleep on red silken sheets, with pillows of a diaphanous blue to hold her slumbering face so true.

The night lamp is switched on to keep her at peace for dreams so sweet as she recharges her energy for another day's meet.

www.ingramcontent.com/pod-product-compliance
Lightning Source LLC
Chambersburg PA
CBHW041737300726
48978CB00001B/22